MW01689301

To LAURAL.

BALANCE IS IN ALL THINGS

Ambrose [illegible]

The Art of Balance

The Art of Balance

San-Datchi Kata

Ambrose Loughlin

1997
Galde Press, Inc.
Lakeville, Minnesota

FIRST EDITION
First Printing, 1997

Photography by Allan McLeish
Cover design by Christopher Wells
Front cover painting: "The Art of Balance" by Ambrose Loughlin, showing Fire (sun), Water (river), Earth (mineral rock), Air (sky and clouds), and Spirit of life and expansion of consciousness (tree with new leaves).

Library of Congress Cataloging-in-Publication Data

Loughlin, Ambrose, 1955–
The art of balance : san-datchi kata / Ambrose Loughlin.
p. cm.
ISBN 1–880090–34–1
1. Martial arts—Training. 2. Karate—Training. 3. Mind and body. I. Title.
GV1102.7.T7L68 1996
796.8—dc20
96–43352
CIP

Galde Press, Inc.
PO Box 460
Lakeville, Minnesota 55044

For my father, who had
faith when I had none.

About the Author

Ambrose Loughlin was born in Scotland in 1955. He started his training in gymnastics with the Forth Port Glasgow boys brigade and in Port Glasgow high school in 1966 under the instruction of David Allen.

He took over teaching the school team at the age of fourteen with his friend and fellow gymnast, Robert Heron, when their teacher left for a new post. He left school at fifteen and took on an apprenticeship in the local shipyard as a plater/shipwright and taught gymnastics at the local youth club in the evening with his brother Billy. When he was eighteen, he joined his first karate club of *shotokai* form, under Sensie George Taft, to complement his balance in his personal training of gymnastics and energy exploitation.

In 1976 he went to work in Guernsey in the Channel Islands, where he taught gymnastics in a youth club run by Dave Fallah, which he took to the Royal Albert Hall in London in 1977 in a show for the Queen's silver jubilee.

He also taught gymnastics in a school and a leisure center assisting Olympic trampolinist, Ian Harris. On his spare nights, he practiced the *shotokan* form of karate with a local club. He also trained in judo, as a guest of a friend, one night a week.

He returned to Scotland in 1979, joined the fire service and decided to train full time in the *shotokan* form of karate where his father and uncle were practicing under sensie Jim Downie, whom he assisted in later years in various clubs.

He ran his first karate club with his father in Quarriers children's home from 1982 until its closing in 1985. From there he traveled and studied various martial arts and has, for the last six years, run a small club in his home town of Port Glasgow with his associate, sensie George Taft.

He retired from the fire service in 1992 and now works as a passive self-defense instructor in Glasgow.

Contents

Acknowledgements

Thanks to—

Sensie George Taft, S.I.o.M.A. (Scottish Institute of Martial Arts), *Shotokai, Aikido, Iaido,* and *Ki*
Sensie Harada, *Shotokai* and *ki*
Sensie Willie Smith, *Shotokai*
Sensie Jim Downie, *Shotokan*
Sensie Tomita, *Shotokan*
Sensie Kenny Taylor, *Shotokan*
Sensie Dave Hazard, *Shotokan*
Sensie Kawazoe, *Shotokan*
Sensie Dave Gllies, *Shotokan*
Sensie Enoeda, *Shotokan*
Sensie D. Thompson, *Shotokan*
Sensie W. Phiminster, *Shotokan*
Sensie Butch White, *Sankukai*
Sensie Scott Steele, *Kalaripayit*, S.I.o.M.A

Introduction

San-datchi kata means literally "three-stance form" and is not meant to be a martial art on its own, but a self-help home training manual to assist in the *karateka*'s own training under their *sensie*'s instruction.

Training regularly with the art of balance helps to counter the stresses of everyday life and is part of a logical formula to a more relaxed, positive, and healthier lifestyle for the entire family.

The *katas* can be practiced in a small area and so can be used at home, work, office, or dojo—building balance and structure in your own art.

San-Datchi kata is based on traditional karate techniques which are taught and understood by martial arts practitioners all the world over, in Japanese terminology.

The physical movements of each particular technique is taught using similar methods, from Scotland to Japan; the difference is in the understanding of the mind behind the physical movement and the metaphysical changes that take place within the central nervous system, the body's chemistry and the physical body itself which you travel and inhabit with complete control.

With practice, *san-datchi kata* becomes a meditation in motion when approached in an aware and relaxed manner. Each *kata* by design is a vehicle to elevate yourself through the meditative planes. Every technique reflects the nature of life itself, because for every action there is an equal and opposite reaction, a yin and yang, a natural balance of physical and universal energy.

The fuel which powers each vehicle, universal energy, we call *ki,* and the controller of each vehicle, the mind/body consciousness.

When the student performs the technique of *oi-zuki* for example, the mechanics of the movement combined with ki breathing and balance of the stance's energy are infused harmoniously to explode and be released at the focusing point of the technique, which in this case is essentially the attacking or defending hand or foot.

Using the body mechanics of *san-datchi kata,* the *karateka* practices balance and relaxation as the physical movements exercise and massage the muscles, joints, and organs, opening the meridian centers and allowing the universal energy of *ki* to flow freely throughout the body.

Ki is the life-force energy inherent in all living things, the pulse of life itself that manifests in motion. The body carries its own *ki* energy through the energy superhighways called meridian lines that run through all of the body. These superhighways contain energy stations called meridian centers, where we store different types of energy for diffferent purposes.

The meridian center that we focus on within this formula is called the *hara,* which is the center of our body and is situated in the lower abdomen, about two inches below the navel. To tap into this universal energy, the student must learn to control his or her breathing within the *hara* and harness the energy of *ki* at this center, so that he/she can learn to distribute *ki* to any and all parts of the body with complete harmony and balance, to flow with the wind, bend with the trees, and move with the power of a wall of water.

The Art of Breathing

This is a formula for a breathing technique particularly suited to martial arts, which indeed has many other benefits.

This formula, with practice and perseverance, will allow the practitioner to produce *ki* at will.

To begin, sit in *seiza* (see page 95) on your heels, with the upper part of the foot flat on the floor, your spine straight with head balanced on top, knees shoulder-width apart, and your hands resting lightly on your thighs.

This posture will balance, center, and focus your body so that the central nervous system is open. Relax when you breathe out and feel your balance settle into its own natural position. Then focus your imagination using the conscious mind and employ this powerful vehicle to drive the cycle of breath around the specific parts of your body until your air's pathway becomes wholly perceptible.

As you inhale your first breath, feel the air touching your skin above the top lip and up through your nostrils. Follow your breath on its internal journey over the top of your head, down your spine, and up between your legs into your *hara*, filling this space from bottom to top with your inhaled breath. This is the central balancing point of your body.

To help achieve this task—that is, breathing down in the *hara*—you should inhale and then drop the diaphragm to its lowest possible position. This action pushes the inhalation into the desired area, namely the *hara*, and with practice, the direct route set out above can quickly be perceived.

Focus the air within your *hara* to the area on the floor between your legs, and using your hips, point your navel upwards to centralize your physical balance. Then, controlling your exhalation, completely empty your lungs, allowing any tension within the mind and body to dissipate in your exhaled breath. Sink further into your balance as you relax more, still projecting your *hara* to the floor between your legs and pointing your navel upwards as your lungs empty. With practice, you may feel the sensation of a heavy ball bearing beginning to manifest in your *hara*.

Repeat this technique for five minutes, keeping the air in your *hara* for four seconds before exhaling, and then build your own comfort zone for your body's own natural balanced timing. With practice, this breathing will become imperceptible as the lower abdomen muscles take form with the solar plexus and this way of breathing becomes as natural as any other.

This breathing technique on its own, if practiced with awareness and fortitude, can be used in daily life to release tension, improve circulation, and balance the inner organs for a positive chemical flow, which in turn allows clarity of thought and a healthy lifestyle.

Using *San-Datchi Kata*

When tying the knot in your belt, relax and tie with *ki.* This helps, with practice, to raise the consciousness to *karateka.* Breathe out, relax, and drop into your stance, projecting your *ki* forward and down, making sure that your front foot is pointed in the direction in which your energy is to flow. Grip the floor with your toes for a solid stance. Change to next stance by driving through your own center (*hara*), staying the same height and bending both legs simultaneously, gathering the energy in the *hara,* ready to redistribute into the next move. *Kata* should initially be practiced slowly and with awareness of the muscle action in your body as it learns to formulate its own physical balance into a flowing movement.

The natural speed should be allowed to manifest at its own pace as the mind and body learn the formula and relax and flow together.

Because the feet are furthest from the head, their position should be perfected from the very start, thus allowing the body to find its own balance very quickly. Practicing *kata* to music has a benefit for some because it can assist in the rhythm of the *karateka.* As with all training, the *karateka* should visualize an opponent when executing all techniques and feel the timing as though in another dimension of the mind.

The explosion should always come from the *hara* first with the physical following, as *ki* from the *hara* flows through you.

Each *kata* should be regarded as an extension of the next in its benefits.

At the end of a training session, with practice and perseverance and a minimum of twenty minutes meditation in *seiza,* the student will gain profound insight through a balanced body and a calmed mind.

Directional symbols for proper foot and stance positions:

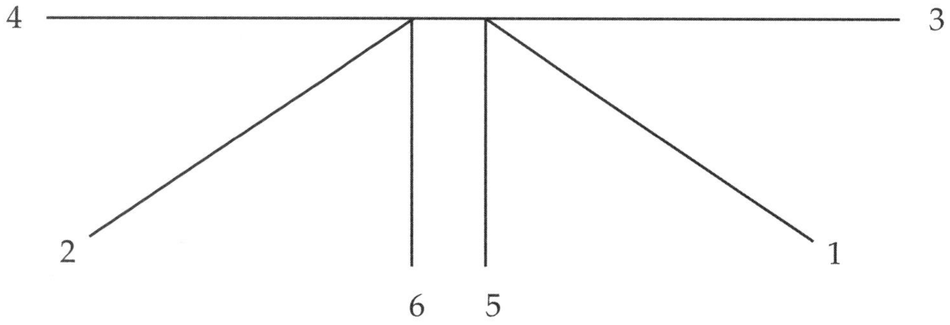

1 and 2, *Zenkutsu-Datchi*
3 and 4, *Kokutsu-Datchi*
5 and 6, *Kiba-Datchi*

Warm-up

Exercises should be performed using the body as a finely tuned machine, the heart working as a hydraulic pump, the veins carrying the hydraulic fluid, (blood) and the muscles of the body acting as hydraulic rams, all focused together with breathing from the *hara* (booster pump).

	Press ups	**Sit ups**	**Leg lifts**	**Squats**
Week 1:	8	8	8	8
Week 2:	16	16	16	16
Week 3:	24	24	24	24
Week 4:	32	32	32	32

Stretching

Starting from the top of the body and working down in logical sequence, completely relax and focus on the internal changes taking place.

Neck: Head forward and back, face side to side, ears on shoulder to shoulder, head circle clockwise then anti-clockwise, alternating four moves each side.

Arms: Circle arms forward, then backward, alternate one forward and one backward. Elbows horizontal with shoulders and throw arms back at shoulder height, then above shoulder height and below shoulder height. Four each.

Waist: Legs shoulder width apart and straight, bend forward and place palm of hands flat on the floor, then bend backward with your hands on your hips and look behind you. Bend to each side alternately, sliding each stretched hand down the outside of your leg. Keep lower body facing forward, twist upper body clockwise and then anti-clockwise. Rotate hips to ease the ligaments and leg muscles, four each side.

Legs: Stand with legs straight and wide apart, bend from the waist and drop your head on to your left knee, swing over to your right knee and then onto the floor in the center, four times each.

Side stretch from same position, bend left knee and sit over the top of your heel, keeping the right leg straight and out to the side with the foot flat on the floor, toes pointing forward, alternate left and right, staying the same height, then same with extended leg, only with toes pointing up, left and right four times.

Sit with legs wide apart and straight, lower chin onto left knee, right knee and forehead on to floor in the center, four times each side.

Kneel down on left knee with the left foot outside the left thigh, right leg extended at right angles, and lower head onto left knee, right knee, and then onto the floor in front, four times each.

Sit in *seiza* between feet and lean back until head is on the floor, using stomach muscles to raise you to *seiza* again, four times.

Sit with legs bent and the soles of the feet together. Holding your ankles, bounce your knees up and down, then pull your ankles into your groin and push down on your knees with your elbows stretching inner thighs, four times.

Sit in lotus position with spine straight, relax, and settle balance. Stand up, circle your knees, press kneecaps back (lightly) and shake off.

When stretching, allow your tensions to be released with your exhaled breath, relax, and drop in to each stretch, hold for four seconds.

San-Datchi No. 1

Stabilizes training stance quickly and efficiently. Builds and stretches hip and leg ligaments and muscles, giving more hip mobility for a bigger and stronger balance. Builds foot and ankle muscles for a strong stance and powerful kicks. Initiates coordination with the separation of the top half of the body from the bottom half, as the top half relaxes and balances on the bottom half and the bottom half learns the physical pattern. Helps open the lower body meridian channels for better internal balance. Allows the mind to concentrate wholly on the foundation of the stance in relationship to breathing, balance, relaxation, and motion. It can be practiced in a small area with logical rhythm and structure.

Yoi

From *yoi,* drop both arms to your side and relax them while turning to face the direction of the stance, *zenkutsu-datchi.* This is at a 65-degree angle left of your center, which allows the feet to be shoulder width apart when facing opponent. Bend the left leg, keeping the lower leg perpendicular and both feet pointing in the direction of the stance (see direction symbols).

Straighten the right leg and, using the right heel as a wedge, feel the energy coming up through the ground as you push down into the hip, keeping the hips square to the body, always exhaling when in motion.

Breathing with *ki,* and your navel pointing upwards, sit down on top of your stance with the upper body relaxed and balanced on top of the hips.

When changing to the right side, all universal joints should be activated in the body, both legs bending simultaneously so that you stay the same height, controlling your energy, and as the left heel now locks in to the floor, the right leg is bent with your shin perpendicular.

Always move the *hara* a split second before the body and allow the physical to follow suit with complete focus, so that you are always in control of your own center and therefore anything within your *mawai.*

Left

Zenkutsu-Datchi

Right

From facing right, turn your head and left foot to point to the left side, without straightening your legs. Point the right foot at a 90-degree angle, relax, and slide into *kokutsu-datchi,* keeping the body as small a target as possible. At this point, both legs should be bent and have the weight of the body distributed equally between them.

Turn and face right, keeping your *hara* in control, turning your feet at the same time as your head and body, pointing your right foot to the right and your left foot at a 90-degree angle in *kokutsu-datchi* right.

Left

Kokutsu-Datchi

Right

Kiba-Datchi (center)

Turn head left to face forward into *kiba-datchi*, turn right foot so that both feet are pointing forward, forcing your knees apart as much as possible, and sit down in your stance, as though sitting astride a horse, with your navel pointing upwards.

San-Datchi No. 2

Works both sides equally. Promotes rhythm. Adds energy of *yin* and *yang* in the hand techniques. Helps open upper body meridians, unblocking the central nervous system. Protects six directions in a semicircle. Builds lower body and upper body and left and right coordination. Tones and stretches upper body. Both sides worked equally for better balance. Helps to control light pain as mind is focused on combined stance, breathing, balance, technique and awareness of the inner feeling or sensations it creates. Focuses on four basic energies; heel through hip to technique, yin and yang as one hand explodes away from your center and the other recoils back in to your center, driving through one's own centrifugal energy, focusing them all together within the catalyst of *ki* energy.

Yoi

From *yoi,* turn toward *zenkutsu-datchi* (approximately a 65-degree angle), with closed hands. Extend your right hand so that your fist is directly in front of your *hara,* about sixteen inches from your body. Raise your left fist to your right ear with your palm facing inward then as you drop in to *zenkutsu-datchi, hara* first, withdraw your right fist in a straight line to your right hip bone at the exact same time as you extend your left arm, leading with your elbow, with your forearm swinging down in an arc until the fist is about four inches above your left knee. This should culminate in a *zenkutsu-datchi,* with the hips and body at a 45-degree angle from attacker, all energy and movement focused in the finished technique, extending from your *hara* and in to the rest of your balance.

Left

Gedan-barai

Right

Turn head to the right, place left arm in front of your *hara,* and at the same time raise your right fist to your left ear. Bending both legs at the same time and attacking with your *hara* first, turn body to incoming attack from the right, recoiling left fist to hip, palm facing up, and leading with your elbow, extend your right arm until your fist is four inches above your right knee, palm facing down.

Turn head to left, raising left open hand with palm facing in to right ear while stabbing right hand, open and palm facing up, to the left, with your right forearm across your solar plexus. Draw your right hand into your solar plexus, still with palm facing up, and at the same time, attacking with your left elbow, allow left hand and arm to stay at the same angle, swing left hand to the left side cutting the air with the edge of your hand, turning your palm to face away from your body, your arm bent at a 90-degree angle, your elbow a fist from your body and fingertips in line with your shoulder.

Left

Shuto-uke

Right

Turn head to right, stab left hand across your body until your left forearm is in line with your solar plexus, palm facing up, left fingers pointing to attack and at the same time cross right hand to left ear, palm open and facing in. Leading with your *hara,* recoil left hand to solar plexus and at the same time, leading with your right elbow, swing right hand around, attacking with the edge of your right hand, keeping your arm bent at a 90-degree angle, your fingertips shoulder height and your elbow four inches from your body, palm facing away, turning in to the stance of *kokutsu-datchi* with the technique of *shuto.* Turn and face the front, swinging your right arm around until it is in front of you, straight out and at forehead height, clearing the way, at the same time withdraw left fist to left hip. Recoil right hand, turn right foot to face forward in *kiba-datchi,* and attack punch to face by exploding the technique in front center of you, fist facing out and forearm at a 45-degree angle to deflect oncoming fist. Kick in with right hip, recoil left fist to left hip, and at the same time block *agi-uke* in *kiba-datchi* with the right forearm.

Left

Age-uki

Right

San-Datchi No. 3

Concentrates on hip mobility and power.

Yoi

From *yoi,* turn head to face attacker from the left angle, withdraw left hand to your left hip and straighten your right arm away from your body in line with your *hara.* Drop your breathing and stance, kicking in with the right heel, bringing energy up through to your hip and *hara* to redirect into your technique, keeping your hips and shoulders square to your opponent, and at the same time recoil your right fist to your right side and explode your left fist across your body, twisting it at the last moment so that the palm of the fist faces down and punching with the two extended knuckles in line with your wrist into opponent's solar plexus with complete timing and focus. Turn head to face right attack, swing round left fist in line with attacker, then, staying the same height, and using all joints as universal to give perfect coordination in the transference of energy from left side to right side, drive *hara* and the technique of *oi-zuki* in *zenkutsu-datchi* through your opponent's solar plexus with complete focus of all energies.

Turn head to face left, bringing left forearm parallel with your shoulders and right forearm parallel with chest, turning in to *kokutsu-datchi,* attack with left elbow until it is horizontally in line with shoulders, extending the side of left fist to target while recoiling right fist to right hip.

Left

Oi-zuki

Right

Turn head to the right and cross arms in front of body, this time with your left forearm parallel with your chest and your right forearm above, parallel with your shoulders. Keeping your body at the same height, turn into right *kokutsu-datchi* and execute the technique of *tettsui-uchi.*

Left

Tettsui-uchi

Right

Turn head to face the front, swinging right arm around, extended to front center at chin height with hand open and palm facing down, and turning right foot to face front in *kiba-datchi,* whip left elbow around in an arc, keeping your forearm parallel with your upper arm. At the same time, recoil right fist, palm facing up, to right hip. Extend left arm, fingers open and palm facing down, and recoiling to left hip, whip right elbow around in an arc, executing the technique of *mawashi-empi* in *kiba-datchi.*

Left

Enpi-uchi

Right

San-Datchi No. 4

Focus on speed and fluidity. Fast, practical self-defense blocks.

Yoi

From *yoi,* turn head to left side and, following the formula in *san-datchi* No. 2, *gedan barai* in *zenkutsu-datchi,* perform the same, only with your block at *chudan* height.

Turn head to face right and, withdrawing your energy to your center, redirect it to *chudan-barai* in *zenkutsu-datchi* to your right.

Left

Chudan-Barai

Right

Turn head to face left with left forearm across your solar plexus and right forearm parallel with your chest. Withdraw your right fist to your right hip inside left arm, and at the same time, using the elbow as a universal joint, bring left fist to shoulder height, elbow four inches from your body and arm bent at a 90-degree angle and turning into *kokutsu-datchi,* execute the technique of *uchi-uke,* turning hand toward face at the point of contact with opponent.

Left

Uchi-uke

Right

Turn head to face right, with right forearm across your solar plexus, fist facing down, and your left forearm parallel with your chest, turn in to *kokutsu-datchi* right and using minimum movement, using the universal joints of the elbow and shoulder, execute the technique of *uchi-uke,* turning hand toward face at the point of contact with opponent.

Turn head to face right, with right forearm across your solar plexus, fist facing down, and your left forearm parallel with your chest, turn in to *kokutsu-datchi* right, and using minimum movement, using the universal joints of the elbow and shoulder, execute the technique of *uchi-uke.*

Turn head to face the front and attack *gedan* kick by punching both fists in the shortest possible route crossing the wrists, left over right, catching the attacker's ankle or blocking and punching the shin, while turning in to *kiba-datchi.*

Draw both wrists in to your chest and drive the technique of *juji-uke* in *kiba-datchi* to the attacking face punch.

Juji-uki

Gedan

Jodan

San-Datchi No. 5

Focus on speed and power. Subtle harmony between technique and stance. Coordination between top, bottom, left, and right.

Yoi

From *yoi,* turn head to face left, extending left hand toward target and right fist on right hip. Drop in to *zenkutsu-datchi* and at the same time recoil your left fist to your hip as you explode your right fist to solar plexus area of attacker, turning fist at last minute so that the palm faces down and contact is with the two protruding knuckles, keeping them in a direct line with your wrist for strength. Hips and shoulders should be square to opponent and energy from the right heel through to the hip should be kicked in to the punch.

Left

Gyaka-zuki

Right

Turn head to face right, bending both legs, turn in to *zenkutsu-datchi* right and at the same time recoil right fist to right hip, palm facing up, and explode left fist to opponent's solar plexus, shoulders and hips square, kicking energy from the floor through to the left heel and into the hips.

Turn head to face the left and gliding in to *kokutsu-datchi,* recoil left fist to left hip and punch across your body for a close-range attacker and stopping fist in line with the left side of your body, using the technique of *kagi-zuki.*

Left

Kagi-zuki

Right

Turn head to face right and, turning in to *kokutsu-datchi* right, recoil right fist to right hip, palm facing up, while executing the technique of *kagi-zuki* with the left fist, palm facing down.

Turn head to face forward swinging your left hand out in front of you at head height and moving in to the stance of *kiba-datchi,* kick in with the right hip and launch your right wrist, palm facing down, under your opponent's jaw, snapping your fist into line with your wrist at the last moment, punching with top of the two protruding knuckles, the energy being redirected from a forward motion to an upward motion with the snap of the wrist and at the same time, recoiling your left fist to your left hip.

Kick in with your left hip and, exploding the left wrist forward, execute the technique of *agi-zuki* in *kiha-datchi.*

Center

Agi-zuki

Center

San-Datchi No. 6

Always return to basic stance before executing next kick. Builds power, strength, and stamina in legs. Focus on redistribution of balance.

Yoi

From *yoi,* turn left in to *zenkutsu-datchi* and, keeping your left leg bent and your foot flat on the floor, drive your hips forward, attacking with your upward pointing right knee and allowing your lower leg to relax and snap out straight with the momentum, extending and attacking with ball of foot with your toes pulled back.

IMPORTANT: Do not allow leg to snap straight, but lock the knee muscles just before the leg straightens completely to prevent damage to the cartilage. Penetrate with your energy through the ball of your foot for just a split second and then snap your lower leg back to thigh with your knee pointing upwards and then place it in *zenkutsu-datchi.*

Left

Mae-geri

Right

Turn head to face right and, turning in to *zenkutsu-datchi* right, driving your hips forward and attacking with your left knee, execute the kick of *mae-eri*, using your arms for balance.

Turn head and body into the stance of *kokutsu-datchi* left, and balancing your weight on your left leg, turn your hips to a 45-degree angle and bring your right knee up to your chest, pulling your big toe toward you and pushing your heel away and using the hip and knee joint, swing your lower leg sideways at a 45-degree angle from your body, attacking with the outside edge of your foot under attacker's jaw in a *yoko-geri ke-agi.*

Turn head and stance in to *kokutsu-datchi* left and balancing on your right foot with your body at a 45-degree angle to opponent, lift your left knee to your chest and allow lower leg to extend into the technique of *yoko-geri ke-ai.*

Right

Yoko-geri ke-age

Left

Turn and face forward in *kiba-datchi* and, keeping your supporting leg bent, lift your right knee and point it to the side with the thigh and the lower leg bent and horizontal, 90 degrees from the side of your body. Drive the right hip forward until the strain is on the muscle at the front of your thigh and then release from the tension, allowing your knee to whip around in an arc, your lower leg extending when your knee is in line with your target and attacking with the ball of the foot, execute the technique of *mawashi-geri.* Recoil leg and place in position of *kiba-datchi.*

Keeping supporting leg bent and foot flat on the floor, lift left knee to point to the side, keeping the lower leg horizontal and in line with your thigh, push the left hip forward leaving the knee behind, causing tension on the front of the thigh and then release your knee and lower leg in an arc executing the technique of *mawashi-geri.*

Right

Mawashi-geri

Left

San-Datchi No. 7

Focus on timing and balance.

Yoi

From *yoi,* turn left and sink in to *zenkutsu-datchi.* Drive your right knee toward target and using the momentum and lift when your knee is at its optimum height, to attack with your left knee, extending your lower leg and attacking opponent with the ball of your left foot as in *mae-geri* in *san-datchi* No. 6, landing back into *zenkutsu-datchi* with as much accuracy as possible.

Left

Mae tobi-geri

Right

Turn head and slide in to *zenkutsu-datchi* right. Drive your left knee to target as a misdirection and at optimum extension, release your right leg and attack opponent with the technique of *mae-tobi-geri,* using your arms for balance.

Turn head to face left and glide into stance of *kokutsu-datchi.* Lift left knee to chest while turning hips at a 45-degree angle away from target and drive kick, extending your foot in a straight line from your hip to target, attacking with your heel and pulling your big toe toward you, hold for a split second, penetrating your energy through opponent and withdraw back to *kokutsu-datchi.*

Turn head and stance in to *kokutsu-datchi* right, raise right knee to chest turning your body to a 45-degree angle away from your target and thrust heel with all energy behind it into the technique of *yoko-geri ke-kome,* hold for a split second and recoil back to body and into *kokutsu-datchi.*

Left

Yoko geri-ke-kome

Right

Turn head and stance forward into *kiba-datchi* and, keeping your right leg bent and foot flat on the floor for stability, raise your left leg, keeping it bent and pulling your big toe toward you, swing it forward and whip your hips around in a clockwise direction at the last moment, blocking the attack with the sole of the foot, then replacing back in to *kiba-datchi.*

Keeping left leg bent, swing right leg forward and around in a counterclockwise direction at the last moment, executing the kick of *mika-zukigeri.*

Left

Mika-zuki-geri

Right

San-Datchi No. 8

Deflection timing and balance.

Yoi

From *yoi,* turn head to face left, right hand outstretched, fingers pointing forward and palm facing down. Raise left arm with upper arm horizontal with shoulder and lower arm above, vertical at 90 degrees and fist facing away from body. Keeping arm at same angle, leading with your left elbow, block attack with the inside of your left wrist, twisting it at the last moment as you turn your hips into a 45-degree angle from your opponent, until palm is facing in, while recoiling right fist to right hip, palm facing up. Elbow should be a fist from your body and left fist should be in line with your right shoulder.

Turn head to face right, point left hand, open and palm facing down toward attacker with right arm horizontal to shoulder and forearm vertical with fist facing away from your body, feeling the torque at your waist, turn in to *zenkutsu-datchi* right, executing the technique of *soto-uke.*

Left

Soto-uki

Right

Turn head to left, point right hand, palm open and facing down to attacker and left fist on left hip, explode in to *kokutsu-datchi* left and block across body with the heel of your left hand.

Turn head to face right swinging left hand around pointing to attacker from the right, placing right fist on to right hip and turning into *kokutsu-datchi* right, execute the technique of *taisho-barai.*

Left

Taisho-barai

Right

Turn head to face forward, swinging right arm, extended around to front center and left fist on to left hip in *kiba-datchi.* Swing left arm in a clockwise direction, blocking the attack with the outside of your forearm across your body while recoiling your right fist to right hip.

Recoil left fist to left hip while executing the technique of *ude-barai* with your right forearm.

Left

Ude-barai

Right

San-Datchi No. 9

Speed and subtle focus.

Yoi

From *yoi,* turn head left to face opponent, extend left arm, fingers pointing to attacker's neck, palm facing down and bring right hand to right ear, fingers pointing forward and palm facing out. Driving forward in to *zenkutsu-datchi,* thrust right hand to the side of attacker's neck, turning hand at last minute and attacking with the edge of your open hand while withdrawing your left hand to your forehead for protection, palm facing away from body.

Turn head to face right attacker and, staying the same height, drive through your center into *zenkutsu-datchi* right, drive left hand, fingers first, to the side of your opponent's neck, turning your hand at the last moment to attack with the edge of your hand while withdrawing your right hand to your forehead, palm facing away from head, executing the technique of *jodan shuto.*

Left

Jodan shuto

Right

Turn head to face left, drop right arm with forearm across chest, fist pointing to target and facing down, withdraw left forearm to sit across right forearm at shoulder height and turning in to *kokutsu-datchi,* attack with left elbow until it's horizontal and in line with your shoulder, allowing the forearm to snap forward and attacking opponent's side of head with back of fist while recoiling your right fist to your right hip, snapping left fist back to chest immediately after contact.

CAUTION: Do not allow arm to snap straight, which will damage the elbow joint, but catch it just before it straightens using the appropriate muscles of your arm.

Turn head to face right with forearms crossed in front of you, left forearm across your chest and right forearm six inches above in line with your shoulders and turning in to *kokutsu-datchi* right, execute the technique of *uraken.*

Left

Uraken

Right

Turn head to face forward and extend right hand to the front, palm facing down and turning right foot into *kiba-datchi,* explode left hand, open and vertical, driving the fingertips through opponent's solar plexus while recoiling right fist to right hip.

Kick through with right hip, exploding right hand forward and executing the technique of *nikite* in *kiba-datchi.*

Left

Nikite

Right

San-Datchi No. 10

Focus on balance, speed, and power.

Yoi

From *yoi,* turn head to face left angle attacker, driving forward and down in to *zenkutsu-datchi.* Keep supporting leg bent and, lifting right knee up to your chest, spin in a clockwise direction until you are facing directly away from your opponent and, using your arms for balance, kick backwards in a direct line from your center, focusing your energy through your heel to target. Do not turn your head to face the target because this will throw your center out and your kick will miss the target. Recoil your knee back to your chest as you spin back around in a counterclockwise direction and back into *zenkutsu-datchi* facing your opponent.

Staying the same height, drive your energy through your center and into *zenkutsu-datchi* right. Keeping your supporting leg bent and foot flat on the floor, bring your left knee up to your chest and spin in a counterclockwise direction, and execute the technique of *ushiro-geri* and back to stance.

Left

Ushiro-geri

Right

Bend back leg and alter feet position to sit back in *kokutsu-datchi* right. Lift right knee up to chest, pulling your big toe toward you and pushing your heel away, drive the edge of your foot down to connect with attacker's lower leg, bring knee back to your chest and place it back in *kokutsu-datchi.*

Turn head and stance in to *kokutsu-datchi* left, and lifting left knee to your chest, execute the technique of *fumi-kome.*

Right

Fumi-kome

Left

Turn head to face forward and stance in to *kiba-datchi.* Lift right knee to left shoulder, allowing lower leg to extend to the area of space at the side of opponent's head above their right shoulder and at the last moment spin your hip in a counterclockwise direction and pull your heel back in a clockwise direction, connecting with the side or back of opponent's head, and back to *kiba-datchi.*

Raise left knee to your right shoulder, allowing your lower leg to snap out to the space above opponent's left shoulder and the side of their head, and at the last moment spin your hip in a clockwise direction, recoiling your heel in a counterclockwise direction, executing the technique of *ushiro mawashi-geri.*

Right

Ushiro-mawashi-geri

Left

The Truth About

Failure: Never be negative about failure. Failure is an extreme measure of learning through our mistakes and can only be achieved through trying. It is better to try and fail than fail to try.

Relationships: A couple should feel free as individuals and reach great heights in common quest. Neither person should feel imprisoned by limitations and boundaries of the other, but make proper use of the magic of love to attain a greater life.

Teachers: Teachers can be helpful along the path of life, but the greatest teacher of all lies deep within, sometimes undisturbed through a whole lifetime. To use this great inner master, simply ask with truth and if you allow, you will be answered with truth.

Messiahs: You are your own messiah. Only you can achieve the great wisdom and feeling of goodness. No one can learn or feel it for you.

Universe: You are the universe manifest in particular form as a direct reflection of itself. You will notice that life revolves around you and not the other way about. Notice the moonbeam reflected on the still waters. It runs in a straight line toward you and even follows you as you walk along the water's edge because you are so important. Or if you look up, down, left, right, in front, or behind you, you will notice that it is you who is in the center of it all.

A good night's sleep: You can never have a good night's sleep when you want one. If you don't want one, you will have it.

Nature: Don't fight nature, become it. The more nature we destroy, the less we have to reflect on; therefore the more unnatural acts take place because of the imbalance.

Reality: Don't see things as they appear, see them as they really are.

Puberty: Puberty is a state of existence of life between child and adult. During childhood, genetic memory is nursed and nurtured by parents to balance the child as much as possible on its way to adulthood. During the states of puberty, like a butterfly from the cocoon, we emerge with new sensitivities, able to take in realized information, creating a new way of learning called "free will." When an adolescent argues with a parent figure, they are really arguing with the genetics inside of their own head, but as it is their parents' genetics they are fighting against, then it is the parents who get the sharp edge of the adolescent's mood changes as they learn to cope with the massive chemical changes within their bodies.

Telepathy: Telepathy is not something we learn. Remember being in a room after an argument and feeling the bad atmosphere? Everyone is telepathic. Telepathy should be nurtured and unfolded, not learned.

Meditation: Everyone meditates, usually without consciously thinking about it. Remember reading a book until the whole world disappeared and it was only yourself in an adventure of the mind? Or when watching the TV until you became part of it and all in the room was outside your vision, until you realized, panicked, and came back to consciousness? Self-thought in mind adventure is a natural meditation path to wisdom.

Knowledge: We all have the same knowledge, but due to our genetic makeup and experience of life, we realize knowledge in different ways. Knowledge is a thing to be "realized" separately, together. I'm not telling you anything you don't already know.

Characters: We all have the same characters which we work with through life, getting rid of the bad or negative characters and replacing them with good or positive, stronger characters. These we work into the conscious mind and collectively call them our personality.

Turning the other cheek: Always greet with good will and positive intentions. If a guest of life shows a nasty or threatening side of their personality, then turn the other cheek and show that you too have an alternative side of nature, always ready to turn it positive at the first opportunity. Never take goodness for weakness; goodness itself is a measure of strength.

Payment: Always pay for your own mistakes. If you don't learn restitution, then you won't learn from your mistakes and you will lose the realization of the knowledge.

Reading: Always read everything twice to realize your understanding of the knowledge.

Life: Life is real, don't fake it.

Giving: Always give on your own terms. If you give on demand, it is no longer a gift but is taken without your blessing and the person who takes becomes a thief of material possession or time.

Anger: Anger blocks the thought process by creating a rush of adrenaline to the brain, shocking the central nervous system. When anger goes, thought returns.

Relaxation: Relaxation is the elixir of life for staying young, alert, fit, happy, and healthy. Relax in every task you perform.

Yourself: You must have time for yourself, have confidence in yourself, and love yourself. How else can you have time, confidence, and love for others if you don't first have it for yourself?

Positive and negative: A positive mind is a builder and moves forward; a negative mind is a destroyer and stagnates.

Imagination: You are your own imagination, and if you put your mind to it you can live it.

Preconception: If you have preconception, you will walk left or right of truth.

The sword: The sword has no skill. The skill is in the master who wields it. Where it comes from and where it goes is of no importance, only that it does.

Glossary of Japanese Terms

San	Three
Datchi	Stance
Kata	Form
Hara	Literally, stomach—internal energy center two inches below the navel
Karate	Empty hand
Karate-ka	One who practices karate
Ki	Life force that runs through all living things
Seiza	Balanced meditation body position; literally, sitting properly
Yoi	Ready
Agi-uke	Rising block
Chudan-barai	Middle body block
Fumi-kome	Downward thrust kick
Gedan-barai	Lower body block
Gyaka-zuki	Reverse punch

Jodan shuto	Upper body knife hand attack
Juji-uki	Double block
Kaqi Agi-zuki	Upward snapping punch
Kiba-datchi	Horse stance
Kokutsu-datchi	Back stance
Mae-geri	Front kick
Mae tobi-geri	Jumping front kick
Mawashi-enpi	Roundhouse elbow attack
Mawashi-geri	Roundhouse kick
Mikazuki-geri	Front sweeping kick
Nikite	Spear hand attack
Oi-zuki	Stepping punch
Shuto-uke	Knife hand block
Soto-uki	Outside block
Taisho-barai	Palm heel block
Tettsui-uchi	Side fist attack
Uchi-uke	Inside block
Ude-barai	Outside forearm block

Uraken	Whip snapping fist attack
Ushiro-geri	Reverse kick
Ushiro mawashi-geri	Reverse roundhouse kick
Yoko-geri ke-age	Side snap kick
Yoko-geri ke-kome	Side thrust kick
Zenkutsu-datchi	Front stance

As exercise gives great benefits to the body, so meditation gives great benefits to the mind.

氣

For other titles of related interest, write for our free catalog.

Send your request to: